Great to Excellent; It's the Execution!

Overcoming the Natural Barriers to Profitable Company Growth

By Jim Alampi

Table of Contents

Acknowledgements and Dedication

This book and The Execution Maximizer™ and The Execution Roadmap© tools are the result of years of research, consulting and business experience. I've truly learned something from each position I've held and from each person I've met or talked to throughout my career.

I'm thankful for the insights of my associates, advisors and affiliates at Alampi & Associates who have provided invaluable assistance to the growth of my company and helped me fine tune the principles set forth in this book and in The Execution Maximizer™ process and The Execution Roadmap© strategic plan template.

My clients and CEO Peer Advisory Group seminar participants consistently challenge my assumptions and strategies and have been an integral part of creating the strategies and tools incorporated in The Execution Maximizer™ and The Execution Roadmap©. I'm incredibly grateful for their confidence in me and for their willingness to adopt my teachings and suggestions. I hope they've benefitted from their affiliation with me.

I've also benefitted from the teachings and advice of some of the best strategic thinkers in my industry, including Jim Collins, Verne Harnish and Patrick Lencioni. My thanks go to each of them. I am also indebted to Vistage International, the world's premier CEO Peer Advisory Group organization, for allowing me to speak over 600 times to members around the world.

Writing this book has been a goal of mine for a number of years and I'm very thankful and appreciative for the writing and editing assistance provided by my writing team.

Meet Jim Alampi

This book is the culmination of decades of my personal experience and learning. I wrote it to share with you the help I've been able to provide executives so they can attain important strategic objectives in their business growth. Everything you read here is a direct result of this experience.

My experience led me to the conclusion that struggling businesses don't suffer from a lack of good ideas, goals or vision. Instead, they tend to suffer from the absence of the tools necessary to focus their businesses, to execute the tasks necessary to achieve their business goals and vision.

In response, I created The Execution Maximizer™ and The Execution Roadmap©, a proprietary process that utilizes the best practices tools from numerous established business innovators, including Verne Harnish, Jim Collins and Patrick Lencioni.

Still, I figured you probably want to know a bit more about just who I am and why it might be worth your while to read my book.

My fascination with organizational dynamics began while I served three years on active duty as an officer in the United States Army, one of the largest and most complex hierarchical- and objective-oriented organizations in the world.

As founder and Managing Director of Alampi & Associates LLC, I've devoted more than thirteen years to coaching CEOs, executive teams and Boards of Directors in the areas of strategy, leadership, execution and business improvement. I've provided advisory services to or spoken before almost 10,000 CEOs and senior executives regarding the lessons I learned as a senior executive at three publicly held companies and as the founder of three start-up companies.

My career has been varied, including work at every type of business – from fledgling privately-held startups to large publicly-held companies. I was the first outside CEO at e-Chemicals Inc., the industrial chemical industry's first B2B e-commerce distributor and supply chain execution provider; Chairman, CEO and President at Insurance Auto Auctions, Inc. (NASDAQ), a $325 million provider of total loss vehicle and claims processing services; President at Van Waters & Rogers Inc. ($1.5 billion), Senior Vice President at Univar Corporation and its subsidiaries (a $2.8 billion NYSE corporation) and Chief Operating Officer at VWR Corporation (NASDAQ $625 million).

As an entrepreneur who has led three professional services start-up companies, I'm keenly aware of the specific needs and hurdles faced by startup companies and I've had to make a payroll – once with a cash advance on a credit card!

Throughout my career, I've gained tremendous insight into the efficient operation of businesses and the predictable patterns that emerge in companies that properly execute their business strategy. My advice, derived directly from these insights, always includes requiring CEOs to ask more questions and give fewer answers, and to create "stop-doing lists" that further focus the executive team's time and energy on the most important and critical aspects of the business.

Using tools set forth in The Execution Maximizer™, The Execution Roadmap© and the concepts you'll be reading here, I've helped numerous CEOs and executives in companies ranging from $25 million to $1+ billion in revenue, all privately-, closely- or family-owned.

I've long been a member of the National Association of Corporate Directors and I've been a director and/or chairman of more than 20 for-profit public and private company boards, chairing four of them.

As a result of my decades of experience, demand on my time exceeds my ability to work with every CEO who asks. It's hoped, by writing this book, I can reach even more

CEOs, executives and teams in need of what I can show them – people like you.

I sincerely hope you implement a few of the ideas and tools as soon as possible. I think you'll thank me when you do.

I suggest you visit The Execution Maximizer™ and The Execution Roadmap© Website at http://www.theexecutionmaximizer.com/resources where you can find free articles, presentations and our forms, including The Execution Roadmap© and others referenced in this book.

Foreword

The Story Behind The Execution Maximizer™ and The Execution Roadmap©

If I were asked to list one skill that's made me a successful executive and an effective, sought-after adviser to boards of directors and senior management teams all over the world, it would be the ability to take complex principles and problems and distill them into simple, easy-to-use information and solutions. The Execution Maximizer™ and The Execution Roadmap© are perfect examples of this distillation process.

These two products of my experience incorporate the lessons I've learned as Chief Executive Officer, Chief Operating Officer and/or President of three public companies and founder of three start-up companies. They also incorporate observations I've made in the course of lecturing to and advising thousands of CEOs throughout the world.

I've learned from my own numerous mistakes as well as from the mistakes of others. What I observed revealed to me that there is a discernible pattern in the growth cycle of companies and this pattern dictates that companies all run into the same predictable barriers. I credit the work of Larry Greiner[1], Ichak Adizes[2], Jim Collins[3] and others for triggering my thoughts around the stages of corporate growth and evolution.

Through these many years of exposure to strategies and tactics, I've concluded that there are three key elements excellent companies have in common that allow them to execute superbly: the leadership team, alignment around goals and a culture of accountability. This learning process led to the creation of The Execution Maximizer™ and The Execution Roadmap©.

These tools are designed to create a clear business execution strategy that provides the focus and framework all companies need to follow, if they're to progress from great companies to excellent companies and sustain their success for generations.

One of my big "A-ha" moments in my own growth process occurred on my second day on the job as President of a $1.5 billion chemical distribution business. I remember I took a few files off of my desk, handed them to my executive assistant and asked her to take care of them for me.

---

[1] *Evolution and Revolution as Organizations Grow*, Harvard Business Review, May-June 1998
[2] *Corporate Lifecycles*, Prentice Hall, 1988
[3] *How the Mighty Fall*, Harper Collins, 2009

Before I even crossed the threshold back to my office, this executive assistant stopped me and reminded me that I had already given her about twenty things to do. She then asked which of those *previous* assignments I'd given her should be put on the back-burner, so she could take care of the new tasks I'd just handed her.

She very pointedly asked, "Do you want me to move one of your previous assignments to a lower priority, work overtime to accomplish the new assignment or reduce the quality of work, so all the assignments can be completed?"

This situation showed me the importance of pinpointing priorities to achieve effective delegation.

To assure that my executive assistant and I were always aligned around my priorities, we implemented a simple A, B, C categorization process for each project or task I assigned to her. The most important projects, known as "A" projects, needed to be completed on the same day they were assigned; less immediate projects, known as "B" projects, needed to be completed within three days; and the least time-sensitive projects, known as "C" projects, could be completed as time permitted.

That interaction, on the second day of my new job, and the simple code we created together, led to seven years of working together without any serious miscommunications or misunderstandings about which projects were of the highest priority.

The companies we've worked with over the past twelve years that are best at execution of their long-term vision and plans do it 90 days at a time – in small, tactical bite-size pieces. This approach is incorporated into The Execution Roadmap©, which requires companies to list their top three to five immediate priorities and the process and accountability for implementing each of them. This straightforward approach allows management to communicate the company's strategic priorities, so each person in the organization knows what's important to the company and understands their role in achieving these priorities. The simplicity of the approach makes accountability easy to determine and easy to track.

A second important teachable moment for me occurred decades ago, when a boss of mine suggested that I should incorporate a seemingly ridiculous question into the annual performance reviews of my subordinate executives. The question he wanted me to add was, "What are 3 things I am doing today that I should delegate to you?"

I didn't immediately appreciate the value of this question. I wrongly assumed no employee would willingly seek out extra work and respond with *any* tasks *they* might be able to handle – so why ask?

My assumptions could not have been more incorrect.

Over the more than twenty years I've been asking employees this question since that moment, not one employee has failed to suggest a task that should or could be delegated to them. This concept of delegation is a key component of The Execution Maximizer™ and The Execution Roadmap©, but there's also a right way and a wrong way to delegate.

Piled High and Deep

Here's an illustration of the concept of properly delegating tasks. Early in my role as President of a $1.5 billion public company, I once returned to my office to find an almost two-foot high stack of papers, all from members of my executive team. It was a pile of customer proposals, each in the range of four inches thick.

This pile was just sitting there, in the middle of my desk. There were post-it notes on each proposal, asking me to read them and let the author know what I thought and what changes I would suggest.

Immediately I knew if I touched that stack of papers and answered *any* of the questions *they* were being paid to answer for me, my future as the President in that company was going to be short-lived. I was also reminded of one of my favorite quotes by General Patton, who said, "Never tell people how to do things. Tell them what to do and they will surprise you with their ingenuity."

Rather than proof-reading their proposals and responding to their questions, I sent their proposals back to them with a simple question on the top – on another post-it note.

It asked, simply, "Is this your best work?"

Sure enough, in a few days the proposals appeared again, but this time they were much thinner. Again, I returned the proposals to my executives, this time with a slight variation of the same question: "Are you *sure* this is your best work?"

Eventually, the executives answered their own questions and they made their own decisions, in accordance with the authority and responsibility delegated to them. In other words, they started doing the jobs they were hired and paid to do.

These are just a couple of the many important lessons I've learned that I've incorporated into The Execution Maximizer™ and The Execution Roadmap©. These tools allow users to benefit from my three decades of experience as a business executive and adviser to and in large multi-national businesses. The strategies and guidance offered in The Execution Maximizer™ and The Execution Roadmap© can be instrumental toward helping a company mature into a sustainable and successful business entity that regularly executes its vision and achieves results.

I'll introduce you to many more of the concepts incorporated into these tools throughout this book and point out, sometimes by example, the results you can expect to see when you utilize them.

As you read this book and prepare to begin utilizing these tools, I would suggest you visit The Execution Maximizer™ and The Execution Roadmap© Website at http://www.theexecutionmaximizer.com/resources where you can find free articles, presentations and our forms including The Execution Roadmap©.

Introduction

America is blessed with an enduring entrepreneurial spirit. This explains the zest this country has always exhibited for creating and inventing new products and services, as well as new methods for delivering established products and services. Add in the burgeoning entrepreneurial enthusiasm growing almost everywhere in the world and you'll find a gigantic assortment of individuals and companies, all with great ideas and a strong vision for each of their company's future success.

Why is it, then, that so many of these companies never live up to their full potential or, in extreme situations, fail completely?

The failure to execute business strategy aligned with the company's vision is a key factor in many companies' lack of growth or failure to flourish.

Fortunately, the lack of an execution strategy is not a fatal flaw. It's actually something that can be easily remedied – if it's caught in time – by identifying a few key barriers every company encounters as a natural result of growth and increased complexity, and implementing the right plan for attacking those barriers when they're approached.

While the impact of the execution strategy will be company-wide, it's not necessary to scrap the whole entity and start over. Significant improvement can be made simply by giving the corporate operating structure a quick little "tune up." After all, it's always easier to tune up your car than it is to replace the engine.

The effect of this "tune up" and the purpose of this book are to help executives like you translate your vision into execution, so you can achieve the results you seek, hopefully without scrapping everything you've built so far. The Execution Maximizer™ and The Execution Roadmap© I've developed are an easy-to-use-and-implement plan of attack designed to properly execute any company's business strategy and vision.

The Execution Maximizer™
How to Move from Vision to Execution

Creating a vision for a company is the easy part of being a CEO. Very few companies fail because they didn't have a business vision. But, just because a company has a clear vision doesn't mean they're set up to effectively execute that vision in a way that profitably expands the business. Without effective execution, it's nearly impossible for a business to achieve concrete and reliable results.

Thomas Edison once said, "Vision without execution is hallucination." Jim Collins, in his classic Harvard Business

Review article, *Building Your Company's Vision*, said, "Visionary companies are about 1% vision and 99% alignment." Having a unique or cutting-edge vision by itself is clearly not a guarantee of business success.

The key to sustainable business success is taking a company's vision and then communicating that vision so everyone in the organization buys into it and understands his or her specific role in the business strategy.

After that, all that's left is executing like crazy. The Execution Roadmap© assists executive teams with the creation of a plan or process for executing their primary business objectives.

Too many companies spend two and three days each year in retreats to come up with grandiose strategic plans that far too often gather dust on a bookshelf during the year. To be useful, strategic plans must be dynamic. There must also be a way to translate all of the long-term visionary elements into practical bite-size pieces that an organization can accomplish in short bursts.

The Execution Roadmap© captures everything from the most strategic to the very tactical on one page. This one-page document can then be used to provide a clear roadmap for executive team leadership as they seek to execute the Company's strategic vision and goals.

Two elements have to be present for great execution. There has to be a vision combined with a process to execute it. You can't cross your fingers and hope execution will occur. Execution is a total system – and when you have both present, the results can be excellent.

PART ONE

Brace Yourself for the Barriers

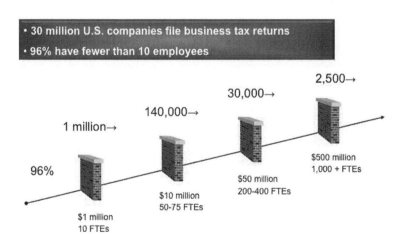

- 30 million U.S. companies file business tax returns
- 96% have fewer than 10 employees

2,500→

30,000→

140,000→

1 million→

96%

$500 million
1,000 + FTEs

$50 million
200-400 FTEs

$10 million
50-75 FTEs

$1 million
10 FTEs

Chapter 1

Barriers Mean You're Growing

All companies experience growing pains as they progress from start-up to established company. You should expect them and welcome these barriers. They're a part of creating a sustainable, growing business. Having a method for approaching these growing pains should be a focus of your business planning from the beginning.

Many executives assume that these barriers or obstacles can't be planned for, that they simply "pop up," based on unpredictable economic or market forces. In reality, these barriers to growth arrive at very predictable times, most commonly based on the number of full-time employees a company has on its payroll.

About ninety-six percent of the 30 million taxpaying business entities in the United States have fewer than ten full-time employees[4]. This percentage has remained static for years. While some businesses remain small because of market dynamics or as the result of a business choice made by the founders, most have the ability and the desire to

---

[4] IRS, Department of Commerce and SBA data

grow, but they've either failed to establish and execute a viable plan or they've been too afraid or disorganized to even try.

Of course, I am assuming you want to profitably grow your business. I occasionally run into a CEO who defines his company as a "lifestyle business," one where growth is not the goal and the owner merely wants to draw enough income to pay for his personal lifestyle. I guess this is okay, although it's a bit like the lesson children learn when they first play video games: the player who stands still gets killed first! Standing still usually means someone is moving past you and I have never found this to be an attractive or sustainable business strategy.

Businesses have three options to deal with changes, just like living organisms do: they can adapt, they can migrate or they can die. Most businesses don't want to die and most can't just pick up and move to a new area, so the remaining choice is to adapt.

Most businesses fail to grow because they can't get past the natural barriers to growth every company must contend with at predictable stages in that growth. The basic barriers to growth fall into three predictable areas: leadership, infrastructure and market dynamics.

Here's how it works:

As companies increase the size of their work force, the requirements for leaping each of these barriers will change. Knowing what these barriers are and having a plan for approaching them that remains true to your vision can mean the difference between a failed start-up and a sustainable business that survives and flourishes for generations.

Chapter 2

Baby Steps

Companies typically grow in a predictable fashion. This is the reason why, with the right approach, the natural corporate barriers to growth can be more predictable than the weather.

The typical start-up begins with one or two people with a great idea for a new business. Oftentimes, the idea is built around a brand new product or service. The beginning stage of a business can be described as exciting and challenging, maybe even exhilarating. But – it's also lacking business processes and is chaotic.

By necessity, the owners are typically involved in each and every aspect of the business at this stage of evolution. They handle everything from the executive decisions surrounding client pitches and marketing approach right down to the most mundane detail of opening and reading the mail, ordering office supplies and reviewing outgoing invoices.

At this point, this all-consuming approach may make some sense. Budgets are usually quite thin at this stage. However, as a company grows – usually after it exceeds ten full-time employees – senior leaders need to delegate some of the tasks and responsibilities that can be better or more efficiently handled by someone else and free them up to work on more strategic issues.

At this stage, executives need to constantly ask, "Is this the best use of my time?", "Is doing this where I contribute the most to my company?" and, "Am I the best person for this task?"

Delegation is difficult for many executives because, after doing *everything* in the business for so long, it's often difficult to trust that someone else will be as invested in the business and think like an owner. It may be difficult or uncomfortable to delegate results desired, but it's also well worth the risk to take that step. Companies without executives who are good at delegation rarely grow past the point of having and retaining 50 to 75 full-time employees.

The problem is that the leaders are so involved *in* the business that no one is focused *on* the business and its future.

Chapter 3

Beyond Ten Employees and ... Barrier One

When a company expands beyond roughly ten full-time employees, it's imperative that it begin to develop an organizational chart that clearly sets forth a chain of command, decision-making responsibilities and functional ownership. It's at this point that most companies create specific titles for specific positions and responsibilities.

At this stage, the number of business titles may be limited to the highest level of senior management. For instance, a company with 25 employees may only have a Chief Executive Officer, Chief Financial Officer and a Sales leader. The rest of the employees rarely have specific titles, because these people still do everything. On a big shipping day, every employee packs boxes. On a big order day, every employee may enter orders.

Even the addition of these few titles, however, helps delineate which decisions must flow through which member of senior management. For instance, an employee with a question regarding new or existing technology might address the questions or concerns to the CFO who, in turn, makes the appropriate decision with or without consultation with other members of senior management.

Chapter 4

75 Employees and Up: Additional Management Levels and Skills Required

To successfully expand beyond 50-75 full-time employees, companies need to add additional layers of middle management. For instance, in addition to a Chief Executive Officer, there may be some Vice Presidents or Directors. Each of these leaders will then oversee a specific department and/or business function.

The organizational chart should expand as the number of employees increase. But, while doing so, we should keep in mind that spans of control (the number of employees reporting to a single leader) have broadened, while the number of levels from CEO to lowest level has been reduced. This is often a conscious effort to increase the speed of information flow throughout a company and to remain agile, flexible and responsive to customer requirements. Bureaucracy, red tape and slow decision-making are barriers to getting to excellent execution.

As an example, one public company's organizational chart I reviewed had 17 levels, from the CEO to the lowest level front-line employee. It has to be almost impossible for the employees at the lowest level of this company to have a clear view or understanding of the company's core values, strategic goals or plans for implementing these goals. In organizations structured like this, employees at the bottom frequently operate based on what they "think" management's expectations are.

To be successful, the vast majority of a company's employees must "know" what management's expectations are, what is important to the company and what their role is in achieving those goals.

Chapter 5

Delegate or Die

If delegation is one of the keys to successful business growth, why do so many executives and companies have such a difficult time doing it?

One reason is habit. When it's something an executive has always done, they often don't bother asking if it's still an appropriate and efficient use of their time.

An example of this is the CEO of a $300 million company who signed each and every check the company sent out. When questioned about why this was necessary, the CEO responded that he had always done that since he started the company and it was his way of monitoring cash flow.

When asked how long ago he'd started the company, his answer was 18 years. It made sense when he started the company, but it no longer did and he'd failed to challenge himself regarding his need to personally continue to sign all the outgoing checks.

This is a great example of something that made sense when a company is in startup mode, has a handful of employees and an extremely tight budget. At some point, the CEO should have delegated check writing authority, below a certain dollar threshold. That threshold should also increase as the company grows and as the CEO gains more trust in the company's employee handling the task.

By the time a company grows to $300 million, the CEO should be signing few, if any, checks.

This seems like a pretty innocent and almost amusing example. However, the downside of this lack of delegation may be monumental.

First, waiting for the CEO to get to the pile of outgoing checks on his desk may slow down projects and tasks across the company. It may create a tense situation between a vendor and the company, if the vendor has to wait long periods between billing and receipt of payment. More important, this activity takes the CEO's attention away from any number of other much more strategic priorities that would have improved or expanded the business, things the CEO should be doing with the time spent writing those checks.

This mandate for delegation is driven by focus and workload. But, consider a third and extreme possibility: what happens if the CEO is hit by the proverbial bus and never again returns to his office? Who in his office knows how to do those things that only he does?

We should be building companies that have redundancy, are sustainable and not dependent on any one individual. In extreme situations, failure to delegate can cause a business to grind to a halt and perhaps even fail.

Chapter 6

More Reason to Delegate

Other reasons for failure to delegate are a lack of trust and the belief by an executive that he or she can accomplish the task better and faster than any employee.

In the former situation, the lack of trust is a no-win situation for the executive. First, if the employee is truly incapable or untrustworthy, it doesn't make sense to pay them and do their job for them. Secondly, if the employee is a capable and trustworthy part of the organization, he or she won't be for long, because employees who are micro-managed become de-motivated and, oftentimes, leave a company for a position elsewhere that gives them actual responsibility.

If delegation doesn't come naturally, what steps can you take as an executive to develop this behavior? First, invest in people who are capable of accepting goals delegated to them and who will hold themselves accountable to get them done. Invest in people who earn and keep trust.

Interviewing, hiring and coaching skills expert Bradford Smart, PhD identified three types of employees: "A" players, "B" players and "C" players. The A player is the top 10 percent of all employees; these are the ones who demand accountability and crave goals. Without direction, these employees will establish their own goals and the means for accomplishing them.

The other 90 percent of employees are divided between B players and C players. B players are the solid core group of employees. C players are those employees who are not and cannot be successful in their current jobs. They avoid blame and accountability as if that's their job.

An executive who can identify the A and B players and invest in them, nurture them and encourage them will find that delegation comes much more easily and naturally.

Chapter 7

Leaders Delegate Goals not Tasks

Once you become comfortable with the process of delegation, you need to pinpoint the goal, to make sure the employee knows exactly what your expectations are. Even the best employees won't be able to execute a poorly-defined goal. Failure to pinpoint the goal might mean that an employee does a great job completing the *wrong* task; they do the *wrong* thing *right*! In addition to being a colossal waste of valuable time, it's also highly frustrating for the employee and for you. And – let's remember – if we don't delegate the goal properly it's our fault, *not* the employee's!

A useful step to help ensure both you and the employee are on the same page is asking the employee to repeat back his or her understanding of the goal that's been assigned. Inevitably, the first time an employee repeats this understanding of the delegated goal, you'll hear it repeated incorrectly. At this point, repeat and clarify what your expectations are and, again, ask the employee to repeat the goal back to you.

This exercise should be repeated until you and your employee are on the same page with a clear understanding of all aspects of the delegated goal.

If, instead, you had merely asked the employee if the goal was understood, the question most likely would have been answered in the affirmative. The misunderstanding wouldn't have been discovered until much later, after considerable time and resources had been wasted.

In addition to clearly defining the goal, executives also need to define what your risk tolerances are. For instance, the employee needs to know if there are any budgetary limitations or customer impact limitations involved in their tasks. You need to make sure the employee knows the kind of negative things that could happen, things you would want the employee to come back to you about and get you involved. You don't want an employee spending weeks going down a blind alley when, if they'd gotten you back involved, you could have helped them get things back on track quickly.

You also need to make the employee responsible for updating you on the progress of the goal. This feedback process is based on the employee's experience and your degree of trust in their ability. If an employee has proven they can handle delegation you might ask them, "Stick your head in my office about every three weeks and give me a one minute update on how you are doing." On the other hand, with a new or unproven employee, you might tell them, "I'd like a five minute sit-down report every Friday morning at 9 a.m. in my office."

The feedback process should be individualized, based on an employee's proven ability to handle delegation. In turn, you need to provide meaningful and timely feedback to the employee throughout the process and after the goal is completed.

Publicly recognizing and thanking the employee for their contribution is an easy, no-cost method of building employee loyalty across the organization and has a great return on investment.

A healthy company culture is one that encourages employees to take on responsibility and be accountable for their actions. It is also one that acknowledges these employees for their contributions and accomplishments. Employees in these types of organizations feel more invested in the success and growth of the business than their counterparts in organizations with a poorly-executed corporate culture.

As an executive, you should be aware that there is a right way and a wrong way to delegate. Following a few simple steps can ensure that you're delegating tasks and authority in the manner most likely to result in the successful accomplishment of the goal.

Chapter 8

Delegation Is A One-way Street...*DOWN!*

An employee's job is to bring solutions and recommendations to senior executives, *not* a litany of questions. Executives who answer each and every question employees approach them with will find a majority of their time is then spent answering increasingly basic and mundane questions.

What happens when you give your employees answers? They will come back for more of them! No learning or growth occurs when we provide answers. The problem is that most entrepreneurs *know* the answers; but our job is *not* giving the people who work for us those answers.

The best seven words I have ever learned, in response to an employee asking me for answers, are, "I don't know; what do you think?"

Employees should be encouraged to seek advice with respect to alternatives, but their job is to bring recommendations and solutions. Employees who are routinely incapable of providing alternatives and recommendations should no longer be serving that role in the company.

Chapter 9

What's Your Question-to-Answer Ratio?

When an employee approaches you seeking quick answers, you should respond with questions, rather than providing answers.

For example, when an employee approaches you with two alternatives for handling a task, it would be easy to simply choose one of the options. But, by asking questions, such as, "I don't know; what do *you* think?" you give employees the experience and confidence to make increasingly more difficult and important decisions, making them *more* valuable to your company.

Your questions shouldn't be nasty or mean-spirited. A solid response might be, "That's a good proposal; did you think about the repercussions if this happened? What is the worst-case scenario that could occur? What would we do if the worst-case scenario *did* happen?"

This is how we should encourage employees to think more deeply and our leaders to learn and grow. Our strength is also our weakness as CEOs and senior leaders; we know the answers most of the time, but *our job is not to give people answers!*

You should periodically measure how many times in a day you asked your people questions, divided by how many times you gave them the answer. My ideal ratio was 20 questions for every answer.

Chapter 10

"What Three Things Am I Doing Today That I Should Delegate to You?"

It's always a good idea to ask your employees, and especially your leadership team, "What three things am I doing today that I should delegate to you?"

This can be done as part of an annual employee review. The obvious upside of this question is that your employees will often help you unload some of the tasks you routinely did, suggesting the ways they're most capable of freeing up your valuable time for more important tasks. You'll also be able to get some clues as to which of your employees might be an A player, B player or C player.

The C players won't be looking for additional responsibility. The B players will likely have some basic recommendations for tasks they can take over. The A players may offer to provide a completely different approach to something that's been done by you a certain way for a number of years.

After all this healthy delegation, you might be tempted to ask, "What's left for me to do?" For tasks that are absolutely mission-critical for the organization, responsibility should clearly still rest with the CEO and senior leaders and proper delegation affords them more time to devote to those tasks. By being too hands-on and overseeing every little aspect of the business, you can actually become a roadblock to the success of your employees and to the growth of the company.

The good news is that the talent for delegation can be developed by following the simple steps outlined above. It's a process that becomes easier the more you delegate.

Chapter 11

The CEO's Job Description

There are four important contributions a CEO makes to an organization that cannot be delegated to anyone else. If the CEO is not driving these four, no one in the company is.

These contributions are:

- The CEO must set the direction for the company.
- The CEO must make sure the right people are hired for the right job and that these employees are being trained, developed and retained by the company.
- The CEO must give employees the resources necessary to perform their jobs.
- When obstacles to employee performance arise, the CEO must remove those obstacles in a timely manner.

In addition to these items, the CEO, working with the senior leadership team, is responsible for setting priorities and deciding what to delegate.

Chapter 12

Your "Stop-Doing" List is More Important than *Any* "To-Do" List

Members of senior management are notoriously poor at identifying things they should stop doing. We typically keep adding more and more to our plates, requiring longer hours and more heroic efforts. I don't know about you, but when I hit 27-hour days, I lose a little productivity!

It is amazing what happens when we empower and encourage our employees to identify things they should stop doing. You may not agree with all of them, but it's amazing how many people spend time creating computer reports for people who stopped reading or needing them years ago! Companies and employees usually have plenty of time to do the work required, if they would only *stop* doing things that were necessary once but are no longer needed or add value to the operation.

Chapter 13

Technology Systems = You Bet the Company

As the number of employees, locations and databases increases, so does the need for increasingly complex systems and structures. Companies with fewer than ten employees generally have basic office systems, such as computers, desks and a telephone system. As the business continues to grow and the number of customers and employees increases, however, the business will need to go through a functional systems evolution, adding new technology systems to make the business run better, faster and more efficiently.

After a few more years, a company is usually operating on multiple hardware and software systems platforms from different vendors, few or none of which interface or work together. Information becomes spread out over different platforms, making it difficult and time consuming to pull together an accurate snapshot of the company and its operations.

At around the time a company passes approximately 50-75 full-time employees, it will often need to adopt an integrated system, or enterprise resource planning ("ERP"), to replace all the functional systems the company has adopted over the years. These ERP systems are expensive, but they can provide tremendous advantages to a company.

ERP is a type of business management software that uses a system of integrated applications to manage all aspects of a company's business, from product development to manufacturing to sales and marketing to finance and human resources. Keep in mind there can be considerable risk in implementing these systems, because they change the way company employees interface with customers and with each other.

That's why this stage of a company's evolution is often referred to as the "you bet the company phase." CEOs and their companies don't implement new, large technology systems frequently, so who in the company has the experience to mitigate risk and control costs? Companies at this size can rarely afford a fully-experienced Chief Information Office (CIO) who has led multiple ERP system integration projects before.

Companies that do not successfully navigate technology systems integration may fail to break through this barrier. Some will fail completely.

As an example of this particular situation, consider a public multi-billion dollar chemical manufacturing company which, in the course of its ERP integration, informed its vendors and customers that they were experiencing implementation difficulties. They then suggested that customers should cease placing orders with them for a period of time, because they could not guarantee the accuracy of their inventory nor did they know how to ship through the new software.

This communication was written by a lower-level employee without senior leadership approval, but it still had a devastating impact on the company. Unfortunately for this company, its customers listened. They stopped placing orders with the company and the company was soon acquired by another, larger competitor.

It's interesting to speculate what this company's future could have been, if they'd handled the ERP integration in a manner more sensitive to client *and* company needs. This mistake also could have been the result of having the wrong person in the wrong position or of giving too much authority to the wrong person.

Chapter 14

Nucor Steel "Bet the Company" and Won

In the 1980's, Nucor Steel was faced with an epic business dilemma that required its executives to determine whether Nucor should "bet the company" on a new steel casting technology. If the risk succeeded, Nucor would become an industry leader and decrease long-term production costs. If the risk was unsuccessful – or if the technology was improved upon in only a few years – Nucor would experience a significant, potentially devastating, financial loss.

In the late 1990s, Nucor successfully utilized the cutting edge technology to build a new steel casting plant and it continues to be one of the largest and leading steelmakers in the United States today.

Chapter 15

Inter-Corporate Culture Clash: Two Opposing Solutions

In an attempt to respond to falling print circulation and the increased use of digital media for news circulation, the CEO at USA Today sought ways to improve the company's bottom line. The goal was to combine businesses and share news content on all the company's print and Internet news platforms.

This concept faced heavy opposition from the management team itself – and from employees who thought the differences in cultures between the print and Internet mediums would be too great to overcome. The CEO felt integration was critical to the future success of USA Today and, to make certain it happened, terminated more than 70 percent of the company's management team to clear the way.

This leader knew that, at the end of the day, it was the CEO's responsibility to set the course for the company and that no strategy – no matter how good – would be effective if the entire senior executive management team wasn't on board.

By retaining and hiring a management team that was aligned with the CEO's strategic plan, it was possible to successfully execute the plan and help USA Today surmount a hurdle to its survival.

The CEO was faced with a time of necessary change in his organization. The intractability of senior management and their unwillingness or inability to change their ways necessitated their exit from the company.

Chapter 16

ERP: Necessary, but Never On time and Never Under Budget

The negative implications of having the wrong people in the wrong position can be enormously significant when integrating a new company-wide technology infrastructure.

Because ERP implementation projects are never completed on time or under budget, the most important piece of advice I can give to companies making such a technology system transition is to invest in your IT department. Get the absolute best IT people you can, even if it means paying a bit more than the company's budget may allow.

CEOs should never delegate this technology system implementation to anyone else; they must ultimately own the project supported by appropriate business and technology experts. These projects are not merely technology projects, they are business projects and the CEO must get involved and stay involved from start to successful conclusion.

When problems arise, which they inevitably will, it will be crucially important for the company to have an expert who can advocate for them and cut through technical jargon, to make sure the company's mission is understood and implemented, so the company's success and bottom line maintains the proper trajectory.

Chapter 17

The Biggest Hurdle as Corporate Systems and Structures Change

One of the primary difficulties in an ERP implementation or any major change in a company is that most people, even the best of employees, are resistant to change.

The typical company change management process involves multiple, predictable stages and emotions:

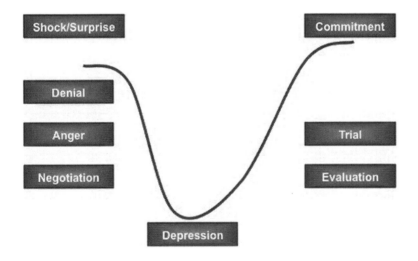

- Shock and surprise as to why a change is necessary and the impact it will have on people's jobs.

- Denial that management will follow through with the new process or system.

- Anger that people have to change.

- Negotiation by certain employees, trying to make the point that they should be able to operate as they always have because their job is unique.

- Depression that the change is going to be implemented and that people's jobs and/or job performance may be negatively impacted.

- Evaluation of the new system by a few employees.

- Trial by the remaining employees as they become resigned to the inevitability of the new system or procedure.

- Commitment to the new system or procedure by all employees as they become convinced that the change is a positive thing after all.

The most flexible and adaptable employees will move through these stages relatively quickly. Some employees get stuck at the anger or denial stage. These employees need to be told respectfully that they need to either get on board with the change or "get off the bus." The departure of a few disgruntled and inflexible employees can also encourage other employees who desire to stay with the company to give the new system or procedure a chance.

It's important that senior leadership doesn't oversell the benefits of any new technology system. They need to clearly explain why the new system is necessary for continued profitable growth and that there will be hard work ahead. The more "buy-in" that is achieved with employees at the start usually results in less resistance that occurs during the project. And, remember the three benefit areas: "What's in it for our customers? What's in it for our Company? What's in it for you?"

Chapter 18

Keeping Resistance to Change at a Minimum

Implementing a significant change in the way a company operates can be made easier if a company evaluates prospective employees for flexibility and adaptability, to imbue the company culture with an appreciation for business growth and improvement through change management.

For example, as companies expand, they often move to new locations. It's important during these transitions that the company's culture and vision be instilled in the employees in the new location. One of the best methods of accomplishing this is to transfer some employees from existing locations to the new facility, so they can set the tone, core values and culture for any new hires at the new location.

Another method of creating a strong, universal company identity and culture is through extensive training of new employees. An example of one company that does this very well is The Container Store.

Early in its evolution, the executives of The Container Store pledged to each other that they would only hire the very best retail clerks, i.e., "A players."

The first step they take, to find this A-player retail clerk, is conducting the lengthy and thorough Topgrading interview, which is deeper and longer – and therefore more expensive – than traditional retail employment interviews.

The second step is offering a compensation package and benefit program to attract and retain the A-player retail clerks. Then, the initial training provided by The Container Store includes a week-long all expenses paid orientation, called "Foundation Week," at company headquarters in Dallas, Texas. This is followed by 270 hours of training during the first year. By comparison, the average retail clerk in the United States receives about seven hours of training during their first year.

The Container Store outspends its competitors in interviewing, compensation, orientation and on-going training, but it boasts an employee turnover rate of less than one-sixth the employee turnover rate in traditional retail stores.

The Container Store realized that finding and retaining one high-quality A-player retail clerk is equivalent to three C-player retail clerks. And, while The Container Store may spend more per employee, they're also hiring and training fewer employees because of their significantly reduced turnover rate. Even after their increased new hire spending, they achieve a very positive ROI.

It should be no surprise that the success rate of new retail store locations of The Container Store is in excess of 90 percent.

Chapter 19

The Impact of Business Focus on the Execution of a Business Strategy

The last barrier to corporate growth is business focus; the sales, operational and financial areas a company must focus on as the business gets larger and more complex.

At the start-up stage, management is usually most concerned with revenue and getting the next customer.

This is the stage where the "three great sales lies" apply: 1) Every customer is a good customer, 2) Every order is a good order and 3) All gross margin dollars are equal. Each of these statements is untrue but, at this stage, a startup company is happy to get any and all revenue from any source!

As companies grow past 10 employees toward the 50-75 employee size, they obviously incur large labor cost increases. This is also the stage where they typically are adding functional technology systems. That hardware, software and training also results in large increases in costs. At this stage, it's critical that someone in the business emerges who is able to balance the company's revenue and cash flow cycles.

As companies grow past the 50-75 employee stage toward the 200-400 employee stage, in addition to managing the revenue and cash flow cycles, they need to focus on the *quality* of the business.

I'm always encouraged to find companies that are good at managing the gross margin line for products, services and/or customers. When I find companies that manage product, service and/or customer quality at the net or contribution margin line, however, I'm ecstatic, because that's where the *real* insight comes.

Companies at this stage should allocate the majority of controllable costs to products, services and/or to every customer, to understand what their true profit is after all the costs-to-serve are included, following receipt of an order. These costs-to-serve include such things as sales rep time per account, accounts receivable, inventory set aside for a customer, special handling, labeling or bar coding, etc.

The goal is not to build a large, complex activity-based-cost model, but rather to identify the large chunks, in relative terms. Precision isn't the goal, but rather to identify, for instance, customers that are unprofitable when you calculate all of their costs-to-serve. So, rather than trying to capture the exact number of hours a sales rep spends per customer per month, create "buckets." The standard might be "A sales rep spends 0-10, 10-20, or 20 or more hours per month with each customer. Again, the goal is not precision but the identification of the least profitable products, services and/or customers, so corrective actions can be taken.

Customer net or contribution margin is one of the most important insights a company can gain as it manages the quality of its business. But, it's also one of the least common metrics I find being tracked in this size of company.

PART TWO

The Rockefeller Habits[5]

---

[5] Titan, Ron Chernow *Mastering the Rockefeller Habits*, Verne Harnish

Chapter 20

Just Three Simple Habits Change Everything

Good news: overcoming the barriers to corporate growth can be as simple as implementing three simple, practical habits. These are the "Rockefeller Habits" for Leadership Teams.

The Rockefeller Habits are simple and common sense:

- Setting the critical few priorities.
- Creating a meeting rhythm for alignment.
- Using data-driven metrics to create accountability and remain focused.

Chapter 21

The Critical Few Priorities vs The Trivial Many

To achieve success and overcome growth barriers, companies must establish business priorities for the next three years, the next one year and – most important – the next 90 days. A leadership team should pick three to five business priorities to be fulfilled during each of these time periods – and the priorities should be interrelated.

For example, the priorities chosen for the 90-day period should be priorities that help the company achieve its one-year initiatives. One-year initiatives, likewise, should help the company achieve its three-year focus areas. Once the 90-day priorities are established, they need to be broken down into priorities on a departmental or functional level and then further broken down into priorities on an individual employee level.

The result is that each employee will have individual goals that are tied directly or indirectly to the company's top priorities. This is about the only way to get every employee aligned toward company goals and spending their time working on the right things.

When establishing company, departmental and individual priorities, it's important to note those priorities should be strategic and mission-driven, not simply tasks that are related to the routine operation of a business. An example would be establishing a budget for the upcoming fiscal year. This is important, but it's an every day or "keep the lights on" part of doing business and *not* a strategic priority that will expand the business and push it through existing barriers.

One of the most important reasons we must tell employees what is important to the company is so they know what to work on. The good news is that A-players know intuitively what to spend their time on; it's why they're A-players! Unfortunately, C-players rarely have a clue where to spend their time so, to gain alignment across the company every employee needs to know clearly what the company's priorities are.

Each employee should end up with individual priorities they can focus on in their job that support the company's priorities. It's the only practical way to gain the alignment Jim Collins talked about when he said, "Building a visionary company requires about 1% vision and 99% alignment."

Chapter 22

A Rhythmic Approach to Leadership Team Meetings

The process of setting and executing priorities for an organization can best be accomplished by establishing and maintaining regular meetings with efficient and meaningful agendas. For effective meetings, agendas should *either* focus on strategic priorities or tactical priorities, but not *both*. The human brain is not very good at flipping back and forth between "blue-sky, creative, out-of-the-box (strategic) thinking" and "hands-on, root cause analysis, problem-solving (tactical) thinking." Great leadership teams declare a meeting will cover either strategic or tactical topics, but not both.

To be useful, information updates regarding progress toward objectives should be provided to executives in *advance* of the meetings, so the information can be reviewed, digested, reflected upon and questions developed. That way, the actual meeting won't be a cursory review of information that could have been read ahead of time. Instead, it can be a deep and lively brainstorming session about the progress of the priorities and troubleshooting of any issues or obstacles that may have turned up.

The value of a leadership team's time together is so high that meetings need to focus on collective intelligence and decision-making.

Chapter 23

Rhythmic Communications: Music that Makes Execution Happen

Companies that don't meet on a regular basis rarely live up to their potential for growth and success. Meetings often get a bad rap and sometimes for good reason. Many executives cringe at the thought of increasing the number of meetings because they think meetings are a waste of time.

In many cases, they're right. Meetings without discipline and without organized agendas directly related to the company's vision and goals can be a colossal waste of everyone's time. On the other hand, meetings that follow a well-thought out agenda and are facilitated can help leadership get a handle on what's happening in the company. They can also keep the employees apprised of leadership's goals and priorities.

As I mentioned earlier, a well thought-out business strategy that's poorly communicated to employees may be worse than no business strategy at all.

The Rockefeller Habits establish a very specific meeting rhythm for executives, including a two-day annual executive team meeting, a one-day executive team meeting each quarter, a half-day executive team meeting each month, between quarters, a 60-90-minute leadership team meeting or conference call each week and a ten-to-fifteen-minute huddle or phone call each day.

This might sound like a lot of time spent in meetings, but assuming the average executive work week is 50 – 60 hours, it amounts to less than five percent of a leadership team's total working hours on an annual basis.

Often, leaders comment that their company is growing too quickly to meet this often. The reality is that, to grow fast, leadership teams need to meet *more* often, because there's greater potential at these times for things to fall through cracks!

The Rockefeller Habits also establish certain agenda criteria, so each and every minute spent in these meetings is directed specifically at establishing the company's immediate, short-term and long-term strategic priorities.

The Daily Huddle's agenda, for example, should be limited to finding out what's up with employees, customers and suppliers, to find out if anyone on the team needs help and then identifying who can help them. The goal is alignment and to eliminate the stupid disasters that occur when people don't know what's going on.

The weekly meeting is the one chance each week for the whole leadership team to be on the same page. Leadership teams that have a standing weekly meeting – on the same day and at the same time each week – actually save themselves time during the week because they know they'll all be together in no more than four days and those routine updates can wait. Obviously, urgent updates need to be handled on the spot.

The monthly meeting is the "no surprises accountability meeting." The worst thing in the world is to set the company's highest 3 to 5 priorities at the start of a quarter and get to the end of the quarter, only to find that several of those goals were not accomplished and no one even knew about it!

The time to learn that a quarterly company priority is failing is *during* the quarter, while there's still a chance to get it back on track. The monthly meeting is for each "quarterly priority owner" to give a status update on the company goal they are responsible for and for the entire team to do whatever is required to get failing goals back on track.

The quarterly meeting includes a post mortem of the previous quarter's goals and the prioritization of goals for the coming quarter. The quarterly meeting should also revisit and confirm or change the company's remaining one-year initiatives.

Every meeting should close with a brief wrap-up of "Commitments and Cascading Messages" – what was decided at the meeting and who in the company needs to know about it.

CEOs need to learn and practice a set of three questions to be utlized any time a leadership team discussion does not end in clear resolution or a decision: "Who owns this? What's the deliverable? By when?" The best leadership teams never leave a topic hanging without a clear path to conclusion.

Larger and more involved items, including prioritizing one- and three-year priorities, analyzing the company's strengths, weaknesses, opportunities and threats (SWOT) and revisiting long-term strategic goals are typically reserved for the two-day annual meeting.

Chapter 24

The Right Metrics Help Companies Evaluate Progress and Remain Focused on Goals

To keep a company moving in the right direction, leaders will need to choose and monitor a combination of standard financial and operational metrics, smart numbers and critical numbers.

Standard company metrics, including financial and operational numbers and ratios, offer a look *back* at what has already happened and offer a basis of comparison or means of measuring past performance. These standard company metrics are often referred to as lagging indicators, because they provide information on something that's already happened and cannot be changed.

Smart numbers, often called leading indicators or early warning indicators, offer a look *forward* at the future. They also provide a mechanism whereby, if the proper smart numbers are chosen, leaders can make some predictions about what might happen in the company's near future.

Smart numbers don't guarantee the future, but they provide some insight about what's around the corner.

Leading indicators are important to monitor because the outcome has not yet been fixed and actions of the leadership team or of the company's employees could positively affect the actual outcome.

An example of a smart number is the "Rig Count" – the number of oil well rigs in operation in the Gulf of Mexico each Friday morning. By monitoring the change in the published rig count from week to week, chemical companies serving the oil industry can project whether there will be increased or decreased demand in this industry segment for chemicals in the future and adjust their plans accordingly.

Another example of a long-range smart number is birth rates that can help construction companies determine whether to expect an increase or a decrease in single-family new home construction over time.

Several companies have released goal or accountability management software packages to allow companies to develop Cloud-based dashboards for the metrics needed to monitor performance across the organization.

PART THREE

Executive Leadership Makes It Happen

Chapter 25

Strategic Execution vs. Strategic Planning

Successful companies aren't necessarily the ones born of the best ideas. The most successful companies are often, instead, those companies that have coupled a good idea with a company vision and a strategic plan to execute that vision. Companies that aren't successful frequently only lack the discipline and focus to execute the vision and strategic plan.

The phrase "strategic plan" brings to mind long, detailed business plans supported by spreadsheets and data that encompass a company's complete strategy for the next decade. However, it's not realistic to implement a ten- or fifteen-year strategy, which is why most of these strategic plans gather dust on executive's shelves. Because they aren't used as an everyday roadmap for the company, it doesn't take long for these strategic plans to become irrelevant to a company's existing and future business.

We've seen many companies that have great strategic plans; the trouble is, they're in a three-ring binder on people's shelves gathering dust. They're often then pulled out at the end of November, when someone remembers there was a plan and now there are only 31 days left in the year to execute it.

If that's the way it's going to work, I wouldn't waste the time or money doing strategic planning because it isn't about the binder and the plan; it's all about executing the plan and getting *results*.

Companies that are really good at executing their long-term vision do it in 90-day tactical, bite-size pieces.

Chapter 26

Success Requires Strategic Execution

Making regular and sound strategic execution a part of a company's strategic process will accomplish a number of important objectives. First, a focus on strategic execution will stimulate dialog and debate between and among leadership, employees and outside advisors. Second, this process will uncover issues and red flags with respect to the company's strategic objectives. Third, the act of focusing on strategic execution will reveal different perspectives and opinions that, in turn, can lead to alternative ideas and scenarios for implementing and achieving company objectives. Lastly, the focus on strategic execution will force discussion on worst-case scenarios and appropriate actions.

Logically, it would seem the important part of this exercise is making the right decision. In actuality, the key to success is taking action and not deferring a necessary action until the perfect answer or complete consensus is achieved.

Many companies and leadership teams get bogged down trying to make the perfect decision, one with no potential for risk or criticism. The complexity of today's business world means we are operating with less information than ever, at a faster pace and where perfect answers are rarely available. All that can be asked is that the leadership team conducts their best strategic thinking about execution, establishes and communicates clear organizational objectives and puts the right people in place with the necessary resources to act on and execute those objectives.

General George S. Patton stated this principle very concisely when he said, "A good plan executed now is better than a perfect plan executed next week." *Companies that are really good at strategic execution define consensus as "I can live with it."*

Chapter 27

Establish One Senior Leadership Team Owner for Each Top Company Priority

Once the leadership team has established the organization's top priorities, each of those priorities needs to be assigned to an "owner" who will be responsible for executing the priority and who will be held accountable for its implementation.

The ownership of a company-level priority should be assigned by matching the requirements of the priority to the leader's particular skill set. Specifically, the priority should be assigned to the person whose knowledge and skill set has the greatest possibility of successfully accomplishing the priority, not just the person who "owns" that function in the company.

The owner of the priority doesn't and shouldn't have to perform all the work required to achieve the priority, but they are responsible for developing and executing the plan to achieve the specific priority.

The first step for the owner will be establishing a plan for execution. This plan will need to:

- Identify who needs to be on the team.
- Establish a reverse project plan, to assure completion by the end of the quarter.
- Establish milestones for the project and dates for completion of those individual milestones.
- Establish meeting and review dates.
- Establish a schedule for updating the leadership team on the progress made toward completion of the priority.

The execution of the plan will require the owner to brainstorm different approaches, appoint group leaders and determine what, if any, additional resources will be necessary to execute the plan and achieve the company objective.

Another important thing the owner of the priority needs to consider is at what point, if any, it's necessary to request assistance from other leaders in the organization.

This consultation with other leaders may be necessary if the project scope or deliverables need modification. In extreme situations, the owner may need to involve the entire leadership team, if the planning and research process reveals that the priority needs to be abandoned because it's unfeasible, if it won't help the company achieve its identified priorities or if it needs to take a significantly different direction.

Chapter 28

Hire Smart People but Focus on a Healthy Organization[6]

Successful companies that routinely meet and surpass barriers operate in a manner that's both smart *and* healthy. Smart organizations have strong experience and skills in the functional areas such as finance, sales and marketing, operations and technology.

These organizations also foster healthy working environments and low employee turnover by eliminating confusion about company goals and politics and by improving employee morale and productivity.

The companies that are able to execute their vision on a company-wide basis are usually adept at hiring the right employees and communicating company priorities, values and strategies to every member of the company team.

CEOs often focus most on hiring smarter, more experienced executives, but that's relatively easy; we can always hire

---

[6] *The Four Obsessions of an Extraordinary Executive*, Patrick Lencioni, Jossey Bas, 2000

smarter people. The real focus needs to be on how to get all the smart people *working together* in a healthy manner.

Unfortunately, too many CEOs think "healthy" involves some warm and fuzzy steps that should be done by the Human Resources department. Nothing is further from the truth! Healthy is actually four leadership steps that every member of a leadership team is responsible for.

The first step is building a cohesive leadership team, which means no C players in a leadership position. The primary reason for this rule is that C player leaders are typically not able to think strategically at the company level.

Another reason to avoid allowing C players in leadership positions is that C-players never hire anything but more C players. Even when they *do* recognize an A-player, they won't hire that person because they'll feel threatened. C player leaders hire more C players and that's a travesty. We should all be hiring people *better* than we are.

Lastly, C player leaders are not fooling anyone. Every employee can identify which leaders fall into the C player category. When a leader hires and keeps a C player in a leadership position, it raises concerns about the leader's ability to attract, lead and develop personnel.

Chapter 29

How Did All the C Players Get In Here?

The only guarantee I know of, in any organization, is that jobs will always outgrow people. The issue isn't *whether* that will happen, it's *when* it will happen. This doesn't mean the employee or leader is a bad person. It usually means that the size and complexity of their job has outgrown that person over time. C players in particular can't easily cope when this happens. The problem becomes even more pronounced when those C players are in a leadership position.

If C player leaders are death to an organization, how do they get the job in the first place? C player leaders almost always fall into one of the following categories:

(1) They were with the company from the start and helped the CEO start and grow it.

(2) They are partners and own part of the company.

(3) They are relatives of the CEO.

(4) All of the above.

To get to the root of this problem, the toughest, most important question leaders should ask themselves is, "Knowing what I know today, would I hire every one of my direct reports tomorrow for the same job?" If the answer to this question isn't an immediate and unqualified "yes," the leader already knows the answer and they need to implement a plan to fix the situation.

Maybe this means reassigning the C player to a position more suited to his or her skill set. Maybe it means getting rid of the C player altogether. Inheriting the wrong person for the job is a common occurrence and there are a myriad of stories of executives having to fire friends and family members because they weren't suited for the job they were hired for.

In some situations, the employee may have been qualified for the job as initially defined, but the job has evolved beyond the employee's interests, education and/or skill set.

These conversations are some of the toughest ones an executive will ever have. But, they must be conducted and in a respectful manner, like this:

"John, I have come to the conclusion that you cannot possibly be successful in your current job. A career is way too precious to waste doing something that you can't succeed at. You've been a strong contributor here in the past and, because of that, let's try to find you another seat on our bus. If we can't find another seat on our bus, I'll help you find a seat on another company's bus. But, I can't leave you where you are."

Too often leaders rationalize keeping a C player because a "warm body is better than nobody." Absolutely untrue! When we tolerate C players, we bring down all of the A and B players. We set a terrible example for other leaders. And, typically, A players will not tolerate having to work with and accept C players and they often leave, since they can always find a job. And, as A players leave, we increase the percentage of C players in our companies, which makes strategic execution even harder!

Putting any one person's welfare above the welfare of the entire company is irresponsible for any leader.

Chapter 30

Create and Over-Communicate the Company's Vision and Goals

Creating and over-communicating a company's vision and aligning the company with its strategic objectives are key components that drive successful strategic execution. Creating this organizational alignment is about qualitative challenges, not quantitative challenges. It requires that companies and organizations establish high levels of trust, encourage positive conflict, keep commitments, require accountability of everyone in the organization and maintain a strict individual and group focus on the objectives that are most important to the organization.

Companies that achieve both smart and healthy organizational alignment are most capable of achieving the company's strategic objectives. To put it simply, successful companies hire and retain quality employees and provide them with quantitative resources and an environment that allows them to efficiently achieve their individual and company objectives.

Chapter 31

You Can't Over-Communicate When Leading an Organization

Establishing and communicating a company's vision and goals is not all that difficult. It begins with the creation of an understandable and up-to-date accountability organizational chart that delineates each department, each employee and each employee's reporting obligations.

Industry experts estimate the average person needs to hear information between 7 and 11 times before it becomes ingrained in memory. That's an average. Some below-average employees may need to hear something *20 times* before it's remembered.

Still, we often underestimate the power of repetition. "We sent them to training so they should have gotten it!" "It's on the bulletin board; are they stupid?" "We sent out an email; what's the matter with our people?"

Companies that do regular employee surveys know that the one item that always shows up as a need is "more and better communication." This employee request will probably show up on every employee survey ever completed for the next 500 years!

The takeaway here is that it's virtually impossible for a company to over-communicate with employees. Providing the same information via different channels and over an extended period of time increases the likelihood that employees will actually remember what you've told them.

Chapter 32

The Power of "MBWA"

One simple communication tool that's been successfully utilized by executives is Management by Walking Around ("MBWA"). This is an unscheduled walk around a facility, stopping by employees' offices and work stations to ask pertinent questions that take the pulse of your company or reinforce goals and values.

This isn't a time where asking a generic, "How are you doing?" will suffice. Here you should ask pointed questions about what's going on in each department and with each employee. This process should involve questions such as, "What does our senior leadership team need to know that we don't?" Or, "If you had my job tomorrow, what's the first thing you would change around here?" Or, "What is the most important thing you're working on and how are you doing with it?"

You need to schedule MBWA; put it on your calendar in 30- or 60-minute blocks. All too often, we have the greatest intentions, but we get busy during the day and, the next time we look at the clock, it's 5:30 PM and everyone has left for the day.

And obviously, during these brief meetings, don't allow employees to ignore the chain of command or try and get you to do something they should have taken up with their immediate supervisor instead.

This is probably the simplest step you could take to increase employee buy-in of company core values and strategies and to stay in touch with how employees are helping make this happen.

Chapter 33

Human Systems Drive Behavior

Establishing human systems that encourage achievement of the company's priorities and goals are critical to alignment, accountability and strategic execution. Your options here include bonuses, incentives, commission plans and performance management goals.

However, you need to make certain that the individual incentives you offer are aligned with the achievement of the company's goals. All too often, I'll go into a company and review its incentive plans, only to find that some people received large amounts, but what they did to earn those amounts didn't support the company's goals. There is misalignment between what is good for the company and what's good for the individual.

Individual performance goals should clearly tie to and support company goals. The only reason to have bonuses, incentives, commissions and performance management goals is to drive *company* goal achievement.

One of the things I hate to hear is when a leadership team tells me they're on target to make the leadership team bonus. That isn't what leaders are on the payroll for! Leaders' jobs are to achieve company goals and, if that happens, the company *might* reward them with a bonus. But *Goal #1 for leadership teams is achievement of the company's goals.*

Finally, watch out for unintended consequences from monetary rewards. People are usually pretty astute at figuring out how to maximize these rewards. Constructing a plan that causes an unexpected negative reaction someplace else is common.

PART FOUR

Your GPS: The Execution Roadmap©

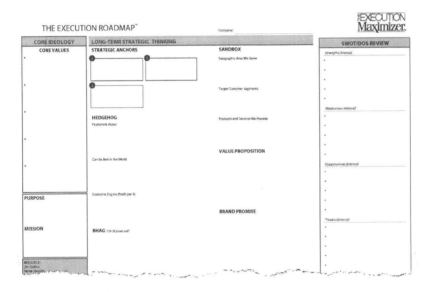

Throughout this section, I'll reference The Execution Roadmap©, pictured above, and provide you with some additional detail about the tremendous value this simple tool brings to your business. To get your own copy of The Execution Roadmap©, visit The Execution Maximizer™ and The Execution Roadmap© Website at http://www.theexecutionmaximizer.com/resources, where you can also find free articles, presentations and our forms, including The Execution Roadmap©.

Chapter 34

Execution is the Fuel for Success

It's no coincidence. "Execution" and "executive" both come from the Latin word "exequi," meaning "attainment" or "accomplishment." A leader's primary purpose is to execute the company's business strategy so the company can attain or achieve its chosen goals.

Achieving this execution is easier said than done, especially when you can often get bogged down in details and minutia or your efforts are hindered by lengthy and out-of-date strategic plans. The Execution Roadmap© allows leaders and employees to keep track of strategic priorities and the steps for implementing these priorities that are consistent with the company's mission and core values.

The Execution Roadmap© conveys all this information on one double-sided document that you can easily have at your fingertips whenever you need a reminder of what the important deliverables are for senior leadership and for the company.

Strategic execution doesn't occur randomly or by crossing our fingers or by hoping it will. It requires two things: a company vision and a *process* to execute it.

To accomplish this seemingly daunting task, The Execution Roadmap© is broken down into the following categories:

(1) Core Ideology

(2) Long Term Strategic Thinking

(3) SWOT Review

(4) Execution and Results

Chapter 35

Getting from Vision to Execution and *Results*

It's easy to explain to a CEO and leadership team that execution is the key to implementing a strategy to achieve desired results. What's harder to understand is how to successfully translate a strategy into execution and results.

There's a process that CEOs of great companies follow that allows them to successfully translate a predetermined business strategy into execution and results. The goal of any strategic execution process is to produce concrete results that enable the organization to make progress toward its envisioned future.

The first step is the development of a comprehensive strategic execution process which, by necessity, is driven by the company's CEO and senior leadership team. This strategic execution process has four individual components:

- Regular and sound strategic thinking.
- Identifying and setting accountability for the organization's top priorities.

- Establishing and maintaining a leadership team meeting rhythm.

- Creating a company vision and alignment process.

These four steps will be the main force that drives the successful execution of a strategic plan.

Chapter 36

Core Ideology; the Most Important Element in a Company's Vision

Core ideology includes the company's core values, purpose and mission. By establishing, clearly delineating and communicating the company's core values, a company is able to establish a framework and structure for the way its employees operate and treat customers, vendors and each other. It also acts as a reminder of what the company's core values are when crucial, heat-of-the-moment decisions need to be made.

Core values establish an identity for the company, so each employee understands which behavior is acceptable and expected.

Core values should be simple – one word and typically no more than four – each defined by a short sentence. Longer value or mission statements are nearly impossible for employees to remember or implement. You can't implement an ideology or value system that you don't easily remember.

If every employee can't remember the core values off the top of their heads, you don't have any. They must be top-of-mind for every employee, every day of every week of every month of every quarter of every year.

The core values are really guidelines for behavior inside the company *and* externally, to the company's customers and suppliers. They should be so important that violating a core value should result in dismissal from the company, without any negotiation or second chances. To have core values that are meaningful, they need to be applied equally to each and every person, so everyone knows and understands no one is immune from complying with the core values of the company.

If, for example, the company's best salesperson violates the core values of the organization, that salesperson *must* be terminated, just like any other employee. Inconsistent enforcement of core values can be deadly to an organization, as employees realize there are different rules for different people. Once this occurs, the company loses employee buy-in to the established company culture and value system.

Having core values that are consistently enforced aids employees in the decision-making process, because they know they can't go wrong if they make decisions in line with the company's stated values.

An important but often-overlooked benefit of enforcing core values takes place during an employee's annual performance review. At this point, a supervisor can evaluate an employee and offer feedback about how their actions did or did not align with the company's established core values. A good question to ask might be, "Give me three concrete examples of things you did in the last year to support our core values."

While dollars and cents, the bottom line and return to shareholders are all very important to successful businesses, it's impossible to overstate the importance of core values. These values tell the company, your employees and the outside world what your company will do and what it won't tolerate. It's how the company will conduct itself in the marketplace. It's the company's reputation and the owner's reputation.

Excellent companies hire and fire for core values.

Strong core values and a good company reputation can create a sense of pride among employees. It can also help to attract new high-quality employees as it helps retain the best of those employees you already have.

Chapter 37

The Elements of Long-Term Strategic Thinking

The long-term strategic elements you need to map out, as CEO, include the company's:

- Strategic Anchors
- Hedgehog
- BHAG (Big Hairy Audacious Goal)
- Sandbox
- Value Proposition
- Brand Promise

Strategic Anchors

A company's Strategic Anchors are the two or three things it does, none of which are necessarily unique, but are put together in a way that creates a competitive advantage for the company. A good example would be Southwest Airlines when it started; its three Strategic Anchors were 1) on-time, 2) low-cost and 3) customer service. None of those were unique, but the way Southwest assembled them together was.

BHAG

The BHAG, or Big Hairy Audacious Goal, is just what the name itself clearly describes – an aggressive and substantial company goal that will be achieved some time over the next 15 to 30 years. An analogy might be if I was in New York and wanted to drive to San Francisco. I would put a huge stake in the ground in San Francisco, which would be my BHAG so, while I was driving the Interstate highway system toward San Francisco, I would never lose sight of the stake in San Francisco. I could also test each turn I made or new highway I entered against whether it would ultimately lead me to San Francisco. I wouldn't want to end up in Toronto or Miami!

Sandbox

Your Sandbox is where you play, usually defined by a geography, customer segment or industry.

Value Proposition

What is it your company does, from a product or service standpoint, that adds sufficient value that your customers are willing to pay to receive? If you didn't add sufficient value from a customer's viewpoint, they wouldn't pay you for it.

Brand Promise

Brand Promise is the quality, performance or price expectation that customers have when they see a company's logo or hear its name. Consider the Mercedes circle logo as an example: most people who see that logo think "excellence," which is their brand promise. What's yours?

Hedgehog

The Hedgehog component of The Execution Roadmap© is a filtering process, to quickly decide which opportunities to say "no" to.

As defined in Jim Collin's *Good to Great*, the Hedgehog analogy is based on the day of a typical hedgehog. Hedgehogs are concerned with and incredibly focused on only the tasks that are important to it. When a predator comes along that interferes with this focus, the hedgehog rolls up into a ball in protective mode until the threat wanders away.

One of the attributes of great companies is that they always know when to say "no." They never waste precious resources chasing opportunities that don't make sense.

It's fine to chase every opportunity, assuming you have unlimited resources. But that's the rub: how many companies ever have enough resources to chase *every* opportunity? Great companies use Hedgehog to define the boundaries for innovation and the kind of opportunities they will pursue, and to quickly say "no" to the obvious outliers.

At its core, the Hedgehog analysis asks a company to define what it's passionate about, what it can be the best at and what drives the company's economic engine. By using the Hedgehog analysis, companies can stay focused on the key areas of their business. Most important, this analysis helps prevent wasting precious resources chasing opportunities outside their "sweet spot."

In my opinion, after Core Values, Hedgehog is probably the next most important element in a company's vision.

Chapter 38

SWOT: Leverage Strengths and Opportunities, Fix Weaknesses and Guard Against Threats

SWOT is a deep analysis of a company's strengths, weaknesses, opportunities and threats. The strengths and weaknesses analysis involves an assessment of what the company does internally exceptionally well and in what areas it needs to improve. An analysis of the company's opportunities and threats involves an assessment of what a company can do externally to generate more revenue and profit and what it should do to guard against threats in its marketplace.

The creation of the SWOT analysis is one of the most important elements of The Execution Roadmap©. A thorough SWOT analysis requires that – prior to the annual strategic planning meeting – senior leaders come up with their own lists of strengths, weaknesses, opportunities and threats. Once compiled, this list may include 25 to 30 items in each category.

You will note that The Execution Roadmap© only allows space for *five* entries in each category. This is because leadership teams need to *prioritize* the top 5 entries in each category; that debate and discussion is really important to alignment among the team members.

Typically the SWOT portion of a two-day strategic planning meeting might take a solid half day to do it right and allow the appropriate depth of discussion.

Chapter 39

Execution and Results

The Execution and Results section of The Execution Roadmap© lists the company's 3 to 5 three-year key strategic focus areas, including metrics for measuring attainment of the goals. There's a section to establish the company's 3 to 5 one-year strategic initiatives, including metrics for meeting these goals. The last portion of this section sets out, on a quarterly basis, the top 3 to 5 priorities for the company in each quarter.

After the SWOT analysis is completed and the resulting metrics have been established, executives need to determine which strengths should be leveraged, which external opportunities should be pursued, which weaknesses need to be fixed, and which of the threats need to and can be guarded against, to deliver the established revenue, profit and productivity metrics within the desired timeframe.

The Execution Roadmap© also provides an accountability mechanism for leaders, to grade the organization on its execution of the company's strategic goals. There is a little rectangular box at the bottom left of each quarterly priority field. Every quarter, a member of the leadership team is accountable for each one of the quarterly priorities.

The circles provide a simple scoring system, to hold leadership and employees accountable. If the quarterly priority was completed, the circle is filled in. If progress was made, but it wasn't finished, half the circle is colored in. If nothing was done on the priority, the circle is left empty. If the priority became irrelevant or was removed during the quarter, a line should be drawn through it.

The Execution Roadmap© provides a framework for distilling the vision and strategic information on the front side of the form into 90-day tactical bite-sized pieces employees and leadership can actually go out and execute. This accountability system also provides immediate feedback for an employee and allows the senior leadership team to quickly look over their priorities and address any employee- or resource-related issues interfering with the achievement of company goals and priorities.

PART FIVE

Recognizing and Creating Effective
Senior Leaders

Chapter 40

The One Roadblock to Overcoming Obstacles

I developed The Execution Maximizer™ and The Execution Roadmap© to help leaders focus on the execution strategies companies need to adopt in order to make the jump from great companies to excellent companies. Inherent in this strategic process, however, is the development of effective senior leadership.

Just because an individual is a competent manager, it doesn't necessarily follow that they'll also be a good and effective senior leader. It's a brutal fact of most business organizations that, sometimes, very good employees and managers are not capable – and will never be capable – of making the transition from manager to senior leader.

These situations can be extremely taxing when an employee has been with the company since the beginning or is one of the CEO's family members or personal friends.

It's at these junctures that the CEO and all of senior leadership need to remember their jobs are to create a strategic plan for the company and to execute that strategic plan by putting the right people in the right positions with the necessary resources to accomplish the company's goals.

In one instance, a CEO agonized over firing an employee who had not grown with the position and could no longer be successful in the position or in the company. The CEO ultimately fired the employee – who happened to be his father – a few weeks before Thanksgiving.

The timing of the termination was bad in and of itself. What made the decision even more difficult was the relationship between the CEO and the family member he had to fire.

Close relationships between the founder or CEO and the initial employees almost always exist in most start-up entities. But, the CEO nevertheless needs to remain focused on his or her responsibility to the company and to each employee. This responsibility should override any feelings of loyalty toward one employee who is no longer capable of being a contributing member of the company. The inability to make these tough decisions is the single largest reason why many entrepreneurial CEOs fail to get their companies to the next level.[7]

While CEOs oftentimes have to make difficult and sensitive decisions regarding hiring and termination of employees, it doesn't mean these decisions need to be handled callously

---

[7] *Why Entrepreneurs Don't Scale*, John Hamm, Harvard Business Review, December 2002

or without any regard to the employee or to their years of service. In fact, it's in the company's best interest for CEOs and all of the leadership team to handle termination of employees in a respectful manner.

Similar to what Marshall Goldsmith says in his book, *What Got You Here Won't Get You There*, the people who get you to a certain level in your company's evolution probably won't be able to get you all the way in your journey.

Chapter 41

How About 360° Leadership Assessments?

Some companies or leaders have utilized what's known as a "360° Leadership Assessment," which is an assessment of a leader by that leader's peers, direct reports and immediate supervisor or boss.

These types of assessments are most valuable when used for developmental and educational purposes only. They can be counterproductive when used for punitive reasons or if they're tied to employee incentives, such as bonuses and pay increases. Nor should a 360° Leadership Assessment take the place of or be used in lieu of an annual performance review.

To be utilized correctly and effectively, a 360° Leadership Assessment should be used as a diagnostic tool, to help executives understand and improve their leadership skills. A well-run 360° Leadership Assessment will provide an executive with a composite analysis of how others view their leadership skills, style and abilities.

One downside of most of these assessments is that, if not well-designed, employees can "game" the system to give a false or misleading picture of an individual's leadership skills. Employees may be overly positive out of fear of retaliation or they may be overly negative, if they have a personal dispute with a particular leader.

The most effective 360º Leadership Assessments are anonymous and use forced choice questions that make it difficult for users taking the survey to "game" the system. The questions should also be asked on the survey in a way that makes it difficult, if not impossible, for the survey taker to determine which trait is being tested by the question.

There are numerous options available for 360º Leadership Assessments, which should be administered by trained and licensed consultants.

To be truly useful, the 360º Leadership Assessment needs to be tied to the strategic goals of the organization. The traits reviewed should be the leadership traits most necessary and applicable to the particular company and to its strategic objectives. While they can be used purely for developmental purposes, the far more important use is for tying leadership behavior to company execution. It's also a great way to define to every leader below the leadership team what leadership behaviors they will need to strengthen to ever be qualified to become a senior leader.

Once a leader has a clear understanding of his or her leadership strengths and weaknesses, including his or her coworkers' perception of their leadership skills, they'll also need to understand how their leadership style impacts – and possibly detracts from – the execution of the company's strategic objectives. Then they'll need to take action to strengthen any areas that may require improvement.

Chapter 42

The Personality Traits of the Ideal Leadership Team

If Hollywood were to script a successful CEO, that individual would be charismatic, daring, confident and completely lacking in any humility or self-doubt. But, in actuality, this stereotype of the successful CEO couldn't be further from real life.

Research has shown that companies that have made the transition from good to great to excellent are frequently run by individuals who, through a strong sense of professional will and personal humility, are able to inspire people to follow them and to buy in to their strategic vision of what is necessary for the organization to achieve immediate and lasting success. These individuals aren't driven by ego, but rather by their belief in and focus on the company, its people and its results.

To illustrate this point, in an article in the Harvard Business Review, best-selling author Jim Collins identified five levels of leadership.

Level One leaders are capable and reliable, easily capable of making productive contributions through the application of their overall talent, skills and reliable work ethic.

Level Two leaders bring their individual capabilities to the table, making the achievement of group objectives happen by working effectively with others.

Level Three leaders are competent managers. They can organize people and resources toward the efficient pursuit of predetermined objectives and keep everything on track.

Level Four leaders serve as effective leaders, with the ability to catalyze commitment to specific objectives and drive the vigorous pursuit of a clear and compelling vision in a way that stimulates higher performance.

Level Five leaders possess all of the characteristics of Levels One through Four. This combination enables them to build enduring excellence through a blend of their unique personal humility and a solid professional will.

What's the biggest distinguishing characteristic between a Level Four leader and a Level Five leader? Level Five leaders understand that *who* they have on their team is more important than *what* the team is trying to accomplish. A Level Five leader knows when the right people are put in the right positions, they can achieve whatever goals the company sets.

Having a Level Five leader at the helm is not a guarantee of success, nor is it the only ingredient required. Companies that have been able to make the transition from good to great to excellent through the execution of strategic objectives usually have had Level Five leaders at their helm. It's also increasingly rare to find a company without a Level Five executive that's able to sustain any amount of long-term profitable growth.

Chapter 43

A Tale of Two Drug Stores

One of the most interesting case studies I can think of involves a comparison of Walgreen's and Eckerd's drug stores.

At the time Jim Collins did his research for his phenomenal book, *Good to Great*, Walgreen's and Eckerd drug stores were both roughly the same revenue size companies. In the time since that study was conducted, Walgreen's has grown into a company with more than $70 billion in revenue, whereas Eckerd Stores ceased to exist after declaring bankruptcy, was bought and sold three times and was eventually split up between CVS and Rite Aid.

So – how did two companies in the same industry experience such different fates? While the answer is certainly complex, it can be boiled down to the fact that Walgreen's had better leadership and a clearly defined, well-executed hedgehog.

Chapter 44

Level Four Leadership is Not Good Enough

Well before its competitors joined the fray, Eckerd Stores was an innovator in the drug store industry. Led by Jack Eckerd – a charismatic leader with a gift for understanding consumer demands and marketing strategies – Eckerd Stores grew from two small drug stores in Delaware to more than one thousand stores spread throughout the Southeastern United States.

Eckerd changed drug stores from tiny, cramped stores that sold medicine and medical supplies into spacious superstores that also sold cosmetics, packaged food, stationary and household goods, in addition to medicine and medical supplies. He capitalized on his southern location – rich with retirees – and offered senior discounts on prescriptions and over-the-counter medication.

Traditionally, drug store photo centers were used purely to attract customers. By adding two-for-one pricing on photographs, to entice vacationers and snowbirds to use Eckerd Stores for their photo processing, Eckerd transformed this part of the business into another profit center.

The store label products offered by Eckerd had a national reputation. At one point, Eckerd Stores was the second largest drug store operator in the United States, with a solid reputation as a quality brand and store.

While there were many things that Eckerd's founder clearly excelled at, he would probably be classified as a Level Four leader. He had a creative genius and undeniable drive for the business, but he didn't necessarily have or recognize the importance of building a strong leadership team. He was the business genius and he surrounded himself with helpers, not leaders.

When Mr. Eckerd became involved in politics, he became less involved in the day-to-day operations of the business. Without a strong leadership team to take over the reins, Eckerd Stores lost its corporate focus, lost sight of what set it apart from its competitors and began to flounder both economically and strategically. This made it an easy target for its competitors.

One thing Eckerd's management failed to appreciate was the value its customers placed on their personal relationship with the pharmacist in the store. That was Eckerd's hedgehog. It was why people entered their store. The leadership of Eckerd Stores was focused on pleasing its shareholders and financial analysts and lost sight of the things that were important to its customers, which were also the same things that had sustained the impressive growth of Eckerd Stores up until that point.

Unfortunately, in the drive to become a diversified conglomerate, leadership lost sight of what really mattered. While its competitors focused on their own hedgehogs, Eckerd Stores made erratic acquisitions of stores and then failed to integrate them to their brand. In some instances, the name of the store wasn't even changed after the acquisition!

Eckerd Stores also expanded its business to include clothing stores, video companies, surgical supply companies and candy companies. This focus on expansion by way of acquisition caused Eckerd Stores to fall behind on technology and riddled it with debt. The debt forced it to slow down and then halt the acquisition of new stores. The lack of technology wasted company and employee time and resources and made shopping at Eckerd Stores frustrating for its customers.

For example, Eckerd Stores didn't begin using computerized scanners at its checkout counters until 1995, something its competitors began doing decades before. This lack of technology and lack of business focus caused further decline in revenue which, in turn, made catching up with respect to new stores and technology economically unfeasible.

Eckerd Stores wasn't done yet, however.

In the 1990s, the company made some improvements to technology that coincided with the increased use of prescription plans in health insurance policies. Eckerd's plan was to capture as much of the insurance carrier business as it could, to improve its lagging pharmaceutical sales.

This was a solid plan and was being executed well. Unfortunately for Eckerd Stores, the insurance carriers wanted to conduct business with drug store companies that serviced multiple states in multiple stores. At that time, Eckerd Stores still only had 1,700 stores in a small segment of the country, while its competitors had a far larger number of stores spread around the United States. For example, Walgreen's had more than 4,000 stores and could therefore service a much larger segment of the population than Eckerd Stores.

The mistakes Eckerd's executive leadership had made over several decades were too engrained and had cost the company too much for it to be able to fully recover. It was eventually acquired by JC Penney & Company and then sold off in pieces to CVS and Rite Aid.

Chapter 45

A Hedgehog, a Strong Team and Level Five Leadership

Walgreen's, unlike Eckerd's, knew what their hedgehog was. Founded by Charles Rudolph Walgreen, Walgreen's leadership, including current CEO, Gregory D. Wasson, is very skilled at building and maintaining a successful leadership team, a group that has bought in to the company culture and hedgehog. This alignment is apparent in each and every Walgreen's store in existence.

Walgreen's hedgehog is customer convenience and each and every business deliverable they execute is measured and tested against whether or not it improves customer convenience. Whereas Eckerd Stores focused on acquiring existing stand-alone drug stores, Walgreen's focused on building more of their own.

By looking at demographics and traffic flow patterns, for example, Walgreen's knows on which corner it would be best to build a new store. Walgreen's also developed and uses only a couple of floor plans for all of its 4,000 stores. The end result is that, no matter where a customer is in the country, when they walk into a Walgreen's store, it feels familiar and convenient. If a customer's out of town and sees two drug stores, one of which is a Walgreen's, they're likely to pick the Walgreen's because they know they can run in and quickly find and grab whatever it is they need.

Walgreen's utilizes some of the same innovations that the founder of Eckerd Stores created decades ago, but also continues to add to this arsenal. Walgreen's was the first drug store discount chain to have prescription pick-up and drop-off windows. Walgreen's also offers a wide array of paramedical services, including flu shots and blood pressure checks. Walgreen's was also the first store to offer in-store photo development machines.

Walgreen's management team knew investing in technology would improve customer convenience. To that end, they installed a satellite system that enabled every Walgreen's store to have access to customer prescription information. Walgreen's also used computer systems to provide real-time ordering and inventory information.

Eckerd's manual sampling of some of its stores meant that it frequently sold out of advertised products. The lack of technology meant that Eckerd Stores couldn't track goods that were stolen or lost and it had a loss rate three times the rate of the rest of the drug store industry. In contrast, Walgreen's employees knew where the products were and they were able to maintain a consistent, reliable inventory for their customers.

Eventually, the technology gap between Eckerd Stores and its competitors was recognized by its customers and led to Eckerd Stores losing customers to its competitors.

Walgreen's has succeeded where Eckerd Stores failed because its leadership team did a better job of knowing what they wanted to do and what they could do well. They created a single, consistent brand that it communicated throughout each of its 4,000 stores around the United States.

Where Eckerd Stores was led by a genius with thousands of helpers, Walgreen's succeeded because it was led by a Level Five executive who understood the value of creating a strong executive team able to implement the company's business strategies. Eckerd's growth approach was scattershot. Walgreen's was hyper-focused and pinpointed on improving and maximizing customer convenience.

Chapter 46

Excellent Leadership and Execution Gets Target Corporation Back on Track

The Eckerd Stores example, while extreme, doesn't mean a company that makes a strategic misstep is doomed to failure, nor does it show that diversification – in and of itself – is a bad thing. One of the benefits of having a strong executive leadership team in place is the ability it gives a company to rebound and recover from a strategy that didn't work out the way it was planned.

If a company remains focused on what it does well and has a solid leadership team in place, it should be able to adapt to changes in its business segment as well as changes in the economy.

One company that exemplifies the ability to pair a well-defined corporate focus with a diversified business plan is Target Corporation. Target's hedgehog or focus is "Department-store inspired service and dime-store inspired value."

Target is the second largest discount retailer in the United States, behind Walmart. Whereas Walmart's target audience is customers seeking the lowest price possible on products, Target understands that its customers want low prices, but they also want to remain stylish and in step with current fashion trends.

One of the most successful recent ventures by Target is aimed directly at their target market. Target's design partnerships, with luxury brands such as Isaac Mizrahi, Missoni and Philip Lim, bring fashion-forward, name brand designs to customers at normal Target prices.

Target has also added grocery offerings, and they experimented briefly with the addition of fresh produce – an experiment that proved too costly for the ROI.

There are a number of challenges with adding a grocery store dimension to a discount retailer like Target. First, the profit margin on grocery items is significantly lower than on the other products Target normally sells. Second, perishable items need to be re-shelved on a more frequent basis, which uses more employee resources and potentially requires hiring additional employees.

The company recently announced it's abandoning its fresh produce, although it will continue to offer an extensive selection of packaged foods, a bump in the road the company was able to notice and rectify before too much damage had been done.

Target's business history hasn't rolled along without some other hiccups along the way. A number of years ago, the company closed more than 250 garden centers because that tangential business line wasn't complementing their core business as a discount retailer of clothing and home goods. The company also found it wasn't able to compete with the rock bottom prices some of its competitors in the discount retail market were already charging for many of the items Target carried.

Because the company was able to quickly respond to these developments, however, the long-term impact on Target's overall business was negligible.

Looking at this from the perspective of a SWOT analysis for Target, it becomes evident the company's strengths include customer loyalty and providing cost-conscious, high fashion choices. Its weaknesses and threats would be the availability of lower-cost items from its competitors, including Walmart. In a down economy or recession, Target may temporarily lose some of its customers to lower priced competitors that can offer similar products.

Target's opportunities include its ability to expand its business as well as continued partnerships with new and emerging designers. Target has also not maximized its international potential, although it has moved one step closer with its acquisition of Zeller, which will provide it with more than 100 retail locations in Canada.

Another opportunity for Target is expansion into urban environments. The traditional Target megastore would, as a general rule, be too costly from a real estate perspective to open in urban environments like New York City and Chicago. The addition of CityStores to Target's competitive arsenal will allow it to rapidly expand its customer base in new market segments.

Chapter 47

Where to Find the Most Effective Leaders

A question frequently asked by CEOs: "Where do I find these Level Four and Level Five executives?"

Surveys conducted by clients studied the turnover rate of employees who were working for another company at the time they were hired, compared to employees who were unemployed and looking for a job at the time they were hired. These surveys revealed that the turnover rate among employees that were recruited away for a position was significantly lower than it was for employees who were unemployed at the time they were hired.

One potential reason for this statistical differential could be that, when an employee leaves a good job situation for a new company, they've already bought in to the company's culture and manner of doing things. An unemployed person, on the other hand, may join an enterprise simply to have a paycheck. Their buy in to the company and their position may be tenuous or nonexistent.

It should actually come as no surprise that the turnover rate among these employees is significantly higher than it is with employees who were recruited into their new positions from other companies. This should not be the deciding point for a hire and may bump against anti-discrimination regulations in certain states. But, the fact is that people who *leave* a job *for* a job appear to stay longer. So, look for your Level Four and Five leaders working in *other companies*.

Chapter 48

You Can't Hire the Best Following the Wrong Process

To ensure that a company hires the best people, the hiring process should be both rigorous and exhaustive. The evaluation process should be extensive, including multiple rounds of interviews, detailed conversations with references and others in the industry, as well as background checks and personality testing.

No employee should be hired if the leadership team isn't completely sure they've found the person who can be successful in the position. It's far better to leave a position empty until the right candidate is found than to fill the position with the wrong person who won't complete the position's responsibilities in a satisfactory fashion. Too many companies seem to think that "a warm body is better than nobody," which is patently untrue.

Once the right people are hired, companies need to do whatever's reasonably necessary to make sure these employees are not, in turn, lured away by other companies. In the unfortunate circumstance where a good employee has been put in the wrong position, the company should attempt to find that employee a position within the company where he or she *can* be successful.

When this is not feasible or where all attempts at reassignment fail, the company should then terminate the unsuccessful employee in a fashion that retains the employee's dignity. By handling terminations in this manner, a company can ensure that most employees who leave involuntarily still leave with a relatively positive outlook on the company and their time as an employee.

In the long run, a thorough recruitment process saves a company time and money. We've already discussed the lower turnover rate which results in lower recruitment and training costs. A thorough interview process will also ensure that a company hires self-motivated people.

This means executives won't need to spend as much time trying to motivate and inspire their workforce. Unnecessary rules and bureaucratic procedures can also be avoided because, when a company hires the right people who are self-motivated and accountable for their actions, fewer rules are necessary to ensure the employee's hard work and dedication.

Chapter 49

A Creative Approach Can Reap Excellent Hires

A great example of how a recruiting process should be used to attract the right employees involved a client in Detroit who was having a hard time finding qualified machinists to hire. In fact, they were having a hard time just finding enough people qualified to *apply* for the positions.

To resolve the issue, the company took out three electronic billboards which were completely blank, except for the words: "hiringmachinists.com". There was no other contact or identifying information.

That company's philosophy was, if a prospective employee couldn't figure out how to navigate the Internet to find the Website, they weren't the type of employees the company was interested in hiring.

Within a week, those three billboards brought in more than 1,500 resumes from qualified individuals interested in applying for the job. These billboards helped the company weed out most of the C players who lacked the motivation to visit the Website to find out about the position. In turn, the company was able focus its hiring attention and efforts on the A and B players that would make the most successful employees anyway.

Another example of a company making hard employment decisions that resulted in a better company occurred after Wells Fargo acquired a competitor. The Wells Fargo executive team knew immediately that the acquired company's management team was not compatible with the Wells Fargo culture or equipped to do the job that Wells Fargo needed them to do. Accordingly, Wells Fargo immediately terminated the leadership team of the acquired company.

Wells Fargo's existing leadership knew it wasn't enough to have the *right* employees; they had to also have the right employees in the *right position*. It was surely a tough decision, but they also understood the importance of having a unified corporate identity, to create a strong company identity and morale.

Post-acquisition integrations can frequently present companies with dilemmas over which employees should stay and which employees should be asked to leave. Figuring this out *during* the acquisition planning and due diligence can help eliminate post-acquisition animosity and can ensure that the acquired company fully integrates into and identifies with the culture and vision of the acquiring company and its senior leadership team. Doing so will allow the new entity to focus on executing the company's post-acquisition business strategies.

Chapter 50

Cultivate Intelligent Risk-Taking and Creative Thinking

Another aspect of creating effective leaders is cultivating an environment where intelligent risk-taking and thinking outside the box are encouraged and where intelligent mistakes are viewed not as catastrophic events but as opportunities for the employee and leaders to learn from experience.

As a founder of a large social media company said to a Vice President who had just admitted making a costly, incorrect decision, "If we weren't making those kinds of mistakes we wouldn't be trying enough new things."

Creativity and innovation cannot exist in work environments where mistakes are viewed as failures, where senior leaders aren't open to suggestions and new ideas or approaches and where there is overly-tight expense control. It's also important to create an environment where robust debate is expected and encouraged.

How companies deal with bad news and errors tells me a lot about that company. *Bad news isn't like wine; it doesn't get better with age*. Great companies regularly and rapidly put the toughest issues on the table first and deal with them.

Positive conflict and the sharing of every employee's perspectives will allow companies to identify all viable options and decide which option works best for the organization and is best suited to help it achieve its goals.

It's unrealistic to think that every meeting will result in complete agreement among members of senior leadership. The goal of these meetings should be to achieve consensus on specific action items. The end result should be a decision that all members of senior leadership can live with and support through execution. As we say, reaching full consensus takes too long in the business environment. Consensus should be defined as, "I can live with it."

At the end of the day, the CEO and senior leadership need to understand that the final decision-making authority rests clearly with the CEO.

CONCLUSION

Chapter 51

Flexibility: Required in All You Do – Now More than Ever

Almost any business can make the journey from good to great to excellent, so long as it has a clearly defined business strategy with a leadership team prepared and capable of executing that strategy. Throughout the process, the business and the senior leadership team need to remain true to the company identity, culture and values.

The strategies and methods I've detailed in this book, in The Execution Maximizer™ and in The Execution Roadmap© are universally useful for businesses of all sizes and in all industries. The equation for success is relatively simple: know your company and your business and make a plan, then execute like crazy.

The economy and advances in technology create a dynamic, ever-changing business climate. Companies that excel will be the companies that have senior leadership teams flexible enough to adapt to these changes.

Companies need to constantly assess and reassess their strategic goals and chart a course for executing a business strategy that results in the attainment of the desired goals. This process requires that companies understand the barriers to growth and are able to use the Rockefeller Habits to overcome these barriers.

Companies need to fully understand their internal strengths and opportunities, as well as their external weaknesses and threats. The most successful companies are able to maintain a laser-like focus on the market they serve and what product or service they are skilled at offering.

Another key component of business success is hiring effective leaders and employees and then placing them in positions best suited to their skill sets. Clarity in communicating the corporate culture, values and goals is also an extremely important element of business success.

Chapter 52

Tight Focus, 90 Days at a Time, Keeps Everything in Perspective

Previous generations of business owners put their long-term goals, execution strategies and deliverables in a lengthy business plan. The goals in these business plans were frequently focused so many years out that it was virtually impossible to come up with an execution strategy that would allow the company to achieve these goals. Further, the long-term nature of the goals made accountability nearly impossible to track.

As a result, business plans were not efficient at guiding companies toward the execution of their strategic company goals. Failure to execute and achieve company goals and strategies decreases the likelihood that companies will continue to grow and remain viable.

The modern approach to strategic business planning, which is best represented in The Execution Maximizer™ and The Execution Roadmap©, forces companies to adopt execution goals that are no further than 90 days out and align the entire company around them.

The CEO and senior leadership team are responsible for communicating the company's priorities to each employee and identifying which employee is responsible for each deliverable. The Execution Roadmap© provides a useful, one-page summary of the company's immediate goals, strengths, weaknesses, opportunities and threats.

The Execution Roadmap© also details who is responsible for each goal, so the senior leadership team can hold employees accountable for those goals. A quick glance at The Execution Roadmap© should provide a snapshot of where the company is at that time and where it would like to be in a few months.

Chapter 53

Preparing for the Future Business Environment Now

When most business owners start their businesses, one of the first things they do is write a business plan, including one- five- and ten-year goals. These are generally lengthy documents that, unfortunately, look too far forward to be of any immediate use. The end result is that most traditional business plans sit on office shelves and gather dust, maybe looked at only once at the end of the year.

It should come as no surprise that traditional business plans aren't the most effective means to accomplish a company's strategic goals, because the goals are generally too long-term. It's not wrong to have a general plan for where a leadership team wants a company to be in five or even ten years. To be truly effective, however, those long-term goals need to be broken down into immediate 90-day goals, with clear and measurable deliverables and accountability.

Business schools are beginning to adapt their curriculum to focus more on immediate results and goals and less on traditional business plans. This movement is gaining acceptance around the country. At an increasing rate, business schools are foregoing traditional coursework that requires students to create business plans in favor of courses that require students to come up with a business idea and then to road test that idea by doing informal market surveys, to fine tune their business approach.

For instance, Harvard replaced their annual Business Plan competition with a New Venture Competition, which gives students the opportunity to use their entrepreneurship principles in an integrative learning environment. Programs like Lean LaunchPad, which is being taught around the country, favor immediate action and feedback to implement business strategies. Some industry insiders are referring to courses like these as the "death of the business plan."

A 2012 study by Bloomberg Business Week analyzed the method of teaching at a select group of business schools. While lectures and case studies represented the most frequently used methods, collaborative projects and experiential training made up between 5 percent and 30 percent of instructional time. It's likely this percentage will increase as more and more companies and business students demand a more entrepreneurial model of business school training.

This entrepreneurial model is in perfect alignment with The Execution Maximizer™ and The Execution Roadmap© because they each encourage the identification of a limited number of short-term objectives coupled with an immediate strategy to execute a plan to achieve those short-term objectives.

Chapter 54

Independent Advisors Can Assist with the Strategic Execution Process

It's often a good idea for companies to utilize independent outside advisers, to help with the strategic execution process. The role of these advisers isn't telling the company what to do or how to do it. Great companies use these senior advisers to give them the cold, hard brutal facts about the company and its current reality.

Some companies also use external advisers as members of their senior advisory board or council that helps the organization as it wrestles with questions and issues that may arise. By retaining independent advisers, an organization can acquire an objective viewpoint that permits it to achieve a higher level of discipline and accountability.

To use an analogy, an independent adviser will teach a company how to fish; it won't catch the fish for the company.

A practical example of the benefit of using an independent adviser as part of the strategic execution process would be a former client who, when the economy hit a bad patch, abandoned its established pattern of leadership team meetings and went into crisis management mode. The result was a gradual loss of alignment between company objectives and strategy. This, in turn, caused a further decline in the company's success.

As their independent adviser, I reminded them of the importance of maintaining the company's strategic execution process, regardless of external happenings. By refocusing their attention on the details of their strategic execution, including maintaining regularly scheduled leadership team meetings, the company was able to weather the economic storm and come out on the other side, poised to take full advantage of opportunities that presented themselves once the economy began to turn around.

It's this ability to maintain the structure of an execution strategy, even in times of business or economic turmoil, that predict whether a company will be able to make the transition from good to great to excellent.

The business environment is cyclical in nature and the period after a downturn is frequently filled with opportunities for exponential business growth. Companies that have maintained their focus and have a strategic plan and the means to execute that plan are able to take advantage of these opportunities. These companies will be at a distinct advantage over companies that have failed to maintain and solidify their business strategies and execution plan.

Chapter 55

Senior Leadership Coaching and the Execution Maximizer™

When facing a barrier to growth, The Execution Maximizer™ process provides direct coaching for a company and its executive team, to equip the team to push through that barrier. After engaging in the Execution Maximizer™ process, companies will have identified and overcome barriers to their growth, successfully implemented the Rockefeller Habits into the organization, developed and communicated their one-page Execution Roadmap© and built a smart and healthy company and leadership team.

Companies and executive teams that want more information or want to get started with The Execution Maximizer™ and The Execution Roadmap© should visit the Website at http://www.theexecutionmaximizer.com/resources.

We firmly believe that CEOs and members of the senior leadership team should never facilitate leadership team meetings. First of all, you cannot be a facilitator and a content participant in a meeting at the same time, and every leader must stay fully engaged in every meeting. The other reason for CEOs not to facilitate is that they usually aren't great at it and they have a much more important role in a team meeting: mining for conflict. The CEO's job in a team meeting is watching for people who are not engaged, listening for tough issues that no one wants to deal with, searching for elephants in the room and assuring that the meeting doesn't end with unresolved issues.

Remember, the three most important questions for a CEO to ask in a team meeting are:

"Who owns this?"

"What's the deliverable?"

"By when?"

About the Author

Jim Alampi

Jim Alampi is Founder and Managing Director of Alampi & Associates, LLC. He coaches CEOs, executive teams and Boards of Directors in the areas of strategy, leadership, executive development and business improvement.

Jim created the proprietary methodology – The Execution Maximizer™ – that uses best practices tools from such thought leaders as Verne Harnish, Jim Collins and Patrick Lencioni.

Alampi is the former President and Chief Executive Officer of e-Chemicals Inc., the industrial chemical industry's first B2B e-commerce distributor and supply chain execution provider. He was formerly Chairman, Chief Executive Officer and President of Insurance Auto Auctions, Inc. (NASDAQ: IAAI), a $325 million provider of total loss vehicle and claims processing services in the United States. He also served as President of Van Waters & Rogers Inc. – the $1.5 billion U.S. industrial chemical distribution subsidiary of Univar Corporation – and Senior Vice President of Finance and Administration for Univar Corporation (NYSE: UVX), the $2.7 billion global distributor of chemicals.

Jim has also led three startup companies, most recently Sales Management Advisors, LLC, which helps sales executives and CEOs create exceptional sales without additional reps, cost or risk.

Alampi has been a member of the National Association of Corporate Directors and has been a director and/or chairman of more than 20 for-profit public and private company boards. He served three years on active duty as an officer in the U.S. Army and earned his Bachelor of Science degree from Rutgers University.

Recommended Reading

The following books and articles have been instrumental in compiling the information that went into this book, and/or they contain valuable tools and methodologies that are essential to a successful strategic execution process:

Burlingham, B. (2007). *Small Giants: Companies that Choose to be Great Instead of Big*. Penguin Group.

Collins, J. and Porras, J. (2004). *Built to Last: Successful Habits of Visionary Companies*. HarperCollins Publishers, Inc.

Collins, J. (2001), *Good to Great: Why Some Companies Make the Leap...and Others Don't.* HarperCollins Publishers, Inc.

Collins, J. and Porras, J. (1996). *Building Your Company's Vision*. Harvard Business Review (September-October 1996, Reprint #96501)

Goldsmith, M. and Reiter, M. (2007). *What Got You Here won't Get You There: How Successful People Become Even More Successful.* Hyperion.

Greiner, L. (1998). *Evolution and Revolution as Organizations Grow*. Harvard Business Review (May-June

1998, Reprint #93308) [originally published in the July—August 1972 issue of HBR]

Hamm, J. (2002). *Why Entrepreneurs Don't Scale.* Harvard Business Review (December 2002, Reprint #R0212J)

Harnish, Verne. (2002). *Mastering the Rockefeller Habits: What You Must Do to Increase the Value of Your Growing Firm.* Select Books, Inc.

Kabacoff, Robert, PhD. *Linking Leadership Behavior and Bottom Line Results.* Management Research Group: http://www.mrg.com/uploads/PDFs/Linking_Leadership_Beh avior_Bottom-Line_Results2012.pdf.

Lencioni, P. (2004). *Death by Meeting: A Leadership Fable...About Solving the Most Painful Problem in Business.* Jossey-Bass.

Lencioni, P. (2002). *The Five Dysfunctions of a Team: A Leadership Fable.* Jossey-Bass.

Lencioni, P. (2005). *Overcoming the Five Dysfunctions of a Team: A Field Guide for Leaders, Managers, and Facilitators.* Jossey-Bass.

Lencioni, P. (1998). *The Five Temptations of a CEO: A Leadership Fable.* Jossey-Bass.

Lencioni, P. (2000). *The Four Obsessions of an Extraordinary Executive: A Leadership Fable.* Jossey-Bass.

Lencioni, P. (2002). *Make Your Values Mean Something*, Harvard Business Review (July 2002, Reprint #R0207J)

Smart, B. (2012). *Topgrading: The Proven Hiring and Promoting Method That Turbocharges Company Performance*. Penguin Group.

Smart, G. and Street, R. (2008). *Who; The A Method for Hiring*. Ballantine Books.

For direct access to information pertaining to The Execution Maximizer™, please feel free to visit www.theexecutionmaximizer.com

For direct access to information about Jim Alampi, please visit the Website of Alampi & Associates (http://www.alampi.com) to see publications, white papers and presentations on all aspects of my business and me.

Made in the USA
San Bernardino, CA
22 November 2013